HIDDEN HISTORY
SPIES

Benedict Arnold

HERO OR ENEMY SPY?

by Aaron Derr
illustrated by Scott R. Brooks

RED
CHAIR
•PRESS•

Hidden History: Spies is produced and published by Red Chair Press:

Red Chair Press LLC   PO Box 333   South Egremont, MA 01258-0333

www.redchairpress.com

Publisher's Cataloging-In-Publication Data

Names: Derr, Aaron. | Brooks, Scott R., 1963- illustrator.

Title: Benedict Arnold : hero or enemy spy? / by Aaron Derr ; illustrated by Scott R. Brooks.

Description: [South Egremont, Massachusetts] : Red Chair Press, [2018] | Series: Hidden history: spies | Interest age level: 008-012. | Includes sidebars of interest, a glossary, and resources to learn more. | Includes bibliographical references and index. | Summary: "He was popular with his troops. And he was such a good soldier that Benedict Arnold became a major general in the Colonial Army. So how did a Revolutionary hero become known as one of the earliest spies in U.S. history?"--Provided by publisher.

Identifiers: LCCN 2017933810 | ISBN 978-1-63440-279-8 (library hardcover) | ISBN 978-1-63440-285-9 (ebook)

Subjects: LCSH: Arnold, Benedict, 1741-1801--Juvenile literature. | Spies--United States--History--18th century--Juvenile literature. | United States--History--Revolution, 1775-1783--Secret service--Juvenile literature. | CYAC: Arnold, Benedict, 1741-1801. | Spies--United States--History--18th century. | United States--History--Revolution, 1775-1783--Secret service.

Classification: LCC E278.A7 D47 2018 (print) | LCC E278.A7 (ebook) | DDC 973.3092--dc23

Photo credits: p. 4: Library of Congress; p. 13: Shutterstock; p. 29: iStock; p. 32: Courtesy of the author, Aaron Derr; p. 32: Courtesy of the illustrator, Scott R. Brooks

Printed in the United States of America

1117 1P CGBS18

Table of Contents

Chapter 1 — An American Hero

On October 7, 1777, Benedict Arnold was ready to fight. Arnold was a **general** in the American Continental Army during the Revolutionary War. He wanted to help the thirteen colonies win **independence** from Great Britain.

But, for the last two weeks, Arnold had mostly been doing nothing. He and his men were just sitting around and waiting for something to happen!

The American soldiers had already fought the British in one deadly battle near Saratoga, New York. The British lost 600 men; the American army lost 300.

After that battle, both sides took a break. The British army had been hoping for extra men to come help them fight. But no one ever arrived. The American army, in the meantime, was getting bigger and stronger as more and more men showed up to help.

On October 7, after 18 days of waiting, Benedict Arnold had finally had enough. The British were moving into fighting position, and Arnold knew the time to strike was now.

Arnold emerged from his tent ready to go. "Victory or death!" he yelled.

Some **historians** believe that Arnold disobeyed the orders of his boss, General Horatio Gates. Others believe that Gates gave Arnold permission to join the fight.

What we do know is, on that day, Arnold led a group of men right into the heart of the battle. He rode his horse between two lines of enemy soldiers, and his loyal men followed.

"Come on, brave boys, come on!" Arnold shouted.

Wounded in Battle

The fighting was tough. Both sides lost hundreds of men. Arnold himself was shot in the leg. When the horse he was riding was also shot, it fell on top of that same leg, crushing it, and Arnold had to be carried from the field.

But he was carried off as a hero. The Americans won the battle, and experts today agree that it was one of the most important moments of the entire war.

Three years later, Benedict Arnold became a spy and a traitor. But it wasn't always that way.

Beginning of the Revolution

When the Revolutionary War broke out in 1775, Benedict Arnold wasn't a general, or even a soldier. He was a **businessman** in New Haven, Connecticut. He and his business partner owned three ships, and they would sail up and down the East Coast buying and selling goods.

He was strongly against the new laws and **taxes** coming from Great Britain. He felt that not only were the laws and taxes not good for his business, they weren't good for the Colonies.

The Sugar Act was passed to force American colonists to send more money to Britain by putting taxes on sugar and **molasses** that was imported into the colonies.

The Stamp Act required the colonists to use special paper from England for their newspapers, almanacs, pamphlets and all legal documents.

Both laws—and others like them—made it very difficult for American businesses to make money.

So Arnold joined the Sons of Liberty, a secret **organization** formed to fight the new taxes. They believed in "no taxation without representation." They didn't want to pay taxes to a government that didn't care about them.

But for Arnold, that wasn't enough. All over the colonies, Americans were preparing for war. Arnold immediately signed up to fight.

He and 59 other men in New Haven, Connecticut, joined a militia—a group of citizens who come together to help the army. Shortly after joining, he was elected **captain** of the group.

On April 19, 1775, the first shots of the war rang out in nearby Massachusetts. "None but the almighty God shall prevent my marching," Arnold said. And so he led his militia into battle.

Famous Sons

Benedict Arnold wasn't the only member of the Sons of Liberty who went on to become famous. Samuel Adams, John Hancock, Benjamin Rush and Oliver Wolcott all signed the Declaration of Independence. And Sons of Liberty member Paul Revere would later be known for his midnight ride when he alerted American leaders that the British were coming.

Chapter 2

Early in the Revolution

In the early months of the Revolutionary War, the Americans were **outgunned**. One thing they needed for sure: cannons. Lots and lots of cannons.

American soldiers carried all kinds of guns and swords to use in battle. But they were mostly good for taking out only one enemy soldier. A cannon could take out dozens with one shot!

Arnold knew of a place called Fort Ticonderoga in northern New York state. Behind the fort's walls, there were cannons and other supplies that would be very useful to the Continental Army. And the fort was guarded by only 48 British soldiers.

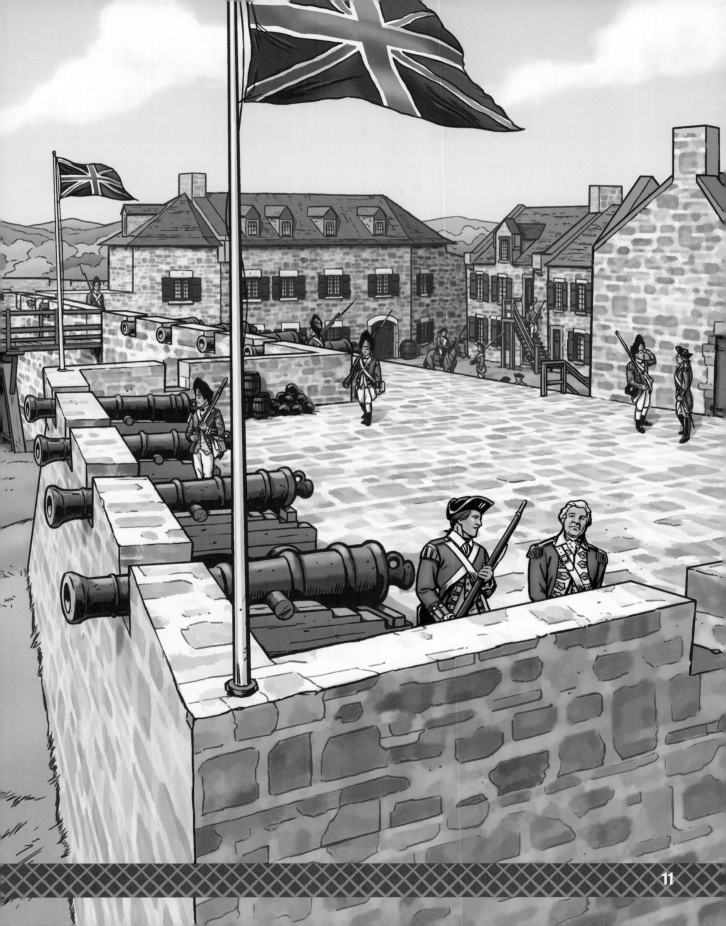

Arnold led some American soldiers to Vermont, where they met up with a man named Ethan Allen, who was in charge of a group of fighters called the Green Mountain Boys. They, too, were going to New York to try to take control of Fort Ticonderoga.

When Allen and Arnold led their men together to take the fort, there was nothing the British could do to stop them. "Come out, you old rat!" Allen yelled to the fort's British commander. He did, and when he saw what he was up against, the British quickly surrendered without a fight.

Cannons for Everyone!

The Americans' victory allowed a large supply of cannons to be sent to the Continental Army in Boston. There, the Americans used them to force the British soldiers to **evacuate**. Arnold had helped the Americans to a huge victory without even firing a shot!

Powder House Day

April 22, 1775, is known as Powder House Day in New Haven. On that day, Captain Benedict Arnold and his men were ready to join the Revolution, but they needed weapons and ammunition. The supplies were stored in a building called a **powder house**, and Colonel David Wooster had the only key. But he wouldn't give the key to Arnold!

"If the keys are not coming in five minutes, my men will break into the supply house and help themselves," Arnold said. Wooster unlocked the door.

To this day, people in New Haven gather together on one Saturday each April and dress in authentic militia clothing to celebrate Powder House Day.

Arnold was feeling great. After Allen and his men left to fight other battles, Arnold began to take charge of Ticonderoga. However, another colonel soon arrived with written orders saying that he—not Arnold—was now in charge.

Arnold was furious! He felt like he wasn't getting enough respect for all he had done to help the Americans. Believe it or not, things would get worse.

A section of Canada called Quebec was home to an important British base. Arnold believed that he and his men could take it. So he asked George Washington for permission to lead an **expedition** to Quebec.

"To Quebec, and victory!" Arnold shouted.

Unhappy Times

After losing command of Fort Ticonderoga, Arnold was so mad that he left and traveled home to Connecticut. It was a tough time for Arnold. When he reached Albany, New York, he received a letter telling him that his wife had died. When he got back to New Haven to spend time with his children, he began to suffer from gout, a disease that causes severe pain in your joints.

The illness would bother him for the rest of his life.

A Run of Bad Luck

The journey was long and dangerous. Arnold and his men were hurt by poor weather, inaccurate maps and their own inexperience traveling through that part of the world.

Of the 1,100 men that left for Quebec, 500 either died or turned back. Arnold knew his force wasn't strong enough to win a fight, so after arriving, he waited for help. Sure enough, Brigadier General Richard Montgomery showed up a few months later with more than 1,000 men. It still wasn't enough.

When they finally attacked Quebec, Montgomery was killed, and Arnold was wounded.

Arnold was brave. He stayed on the battlefield, encouraging his men to keep fighting. But they were greatly outnumbered. Eventually, Arnold was replaced as the leader of the group, and he and his men were forced to retreat.

But Arnold still had work to do. In October 1776, at the Battle of Valcour Island on Lake Champlain, he fought the British just long enough to give American forces in New York time to build their defenses.

Arnold had made some friends in the American military. George Washington seemed to respect him, and Horatio Gates spoke highly of Arnold's actions during that time. However, Benedict Arnold was also making some enemies.

"Money is this man's God," said officer John Brown, "and to get enough of it he would sacrifice his country."

Chapter 3

Fighting On

Less than a year after his return from Canada, Arnold learned that he would not get a **promotion**. Can you guess how that made him feel?

Right! He was mad. Again.

He was so mad, in fact, that he tried to resign from the military. But George Washington didn't want to lose his services, so he convinced Arnold to stay on. Good thing he did.

As Arnold was traveling to Philadelphia, he heard that British soldiers had marched to Danbury, Connecticut. Once there, the British chased off a small group of American troops, and then destroyed a valuable **stash** of Continental Army supplies.

Thousands of barrels of food. Thousands of pairs of shoes. And more than 1,000 tents. All destroyed by the British.

Talk about making Benedict Arnold mad!

Arnold quickly gathered a group of soldiers to fight the British as they tried to return to their ships on the coast. He set up a barricade in the town of Ridgefield. Around noon on April 27, 1777, the British arrived.

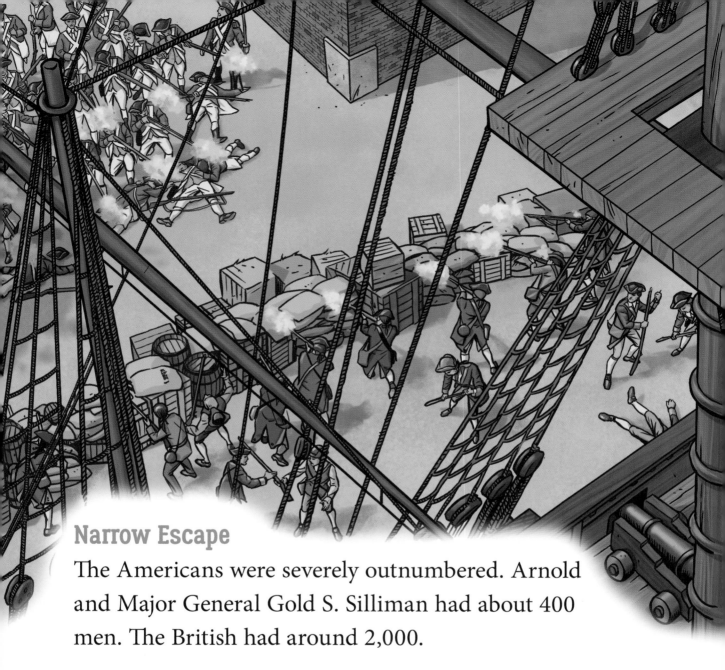

Narrow Escape

The Americans were severely outnumbered. Arnold and Major General Gold S. Silliman had about 400 men. The British had around 2,000.

But the Americans fought bravely, like they always did under Arnold's command.

For one hour, the British hit the Americans with everything they had. But still the Americans didn't move.

The British major general, William Tryon, sent two groups of soldiers to fight the Americans at the very edge of their barricade. But Arnold's men had expected this and were there to fight them off.

Finally, Tryon ordered his men to advance right at the Americans, including a row of 600 men right down the middle. The Americans were in trouble. Arnold ordered his men to **withdraw**.

As Arnold was sitting on his horse between his men and the advancing enemies, the horse was shot and fell on top of Arnold. It wasn't the last time that would happen.

With Arnold lying helpless on the ground, a British soldier charged him and commanded him to surrender.

"Not yet," said Arnold, as he shot and killed his enemy. He then escaped with his men to fight another day.

Back in Business

But Arnold was still not happy. He had been promoted to major general, but he felt that many other military leaders had been unfairly promoted ahead of him.

Once again, Arnold tried to resign. But then he found out that the British Army had recaptured Fort Ticonderoga, and he knew he couldn't give up yet. George Washington himself recommended that Arnold be sent to try to fight the British off.

Arnold was asked to defend nearby Fort Stanwix, which was under attack from British forces. However, Arnold knew he was outnumbered and couldn't win a straight up fight. So he decided to try to trick the enemy instead.

He began to spread rumors that a much larger American force would be arriving. The plan worked, as the British forces abandoned their siege the next day.

Soon after, Arnold joined a group of soldiers under the command of General Horatio Gates and marched to Saratoga, New York, where they would participate in one of the most important American victories of the entire war.

But Gates and Arnold didn't always get along. Arnold wanted to charge into the fight. Gates wanted to set up a strong defense and wait and see what the British would do. Some of the men became loyal to Gates. Others sided with Arnold.

When Gates **filed** an official
report with Congress after the first battle near
Saratoga, he didn't even mention Arnold's heroics.
But, after the two-week break in October 1777, he
couldn't ignore what Arnold did in the next battle,
leading his men into the heart of the fight to secure
victory.

Chapter 4

Arnold the Spy

After suffering the final injury to his leg in October 1777, Arnold was sent to the hospital to recover. But his leg was ruined. He would never be the same.

He also began to grow more and more angry with the leaders of the thirteen colonies. He didn't like the way members of the **Continental Congress** were handling things, and he didn't like the way they were treating him. For many reasons, Arnold was not popular with the members of Congress.

In a letter to General Nathanael Greene, Arnold wrote that the colonies were headed for "impending ruin" if things didn't change soon.

Some members of Congress said Arnold should be in trouble for the way he spent the army's money during the attack on Quebec. The American generals were each given money to use for the war, but Arnold was unable to provide proof of how he spent his share of that money.

Arnold had no way to prove that he didn't take the money for himself. As pressure mounted on him, it was then that Arnold made the decision to become a spy and give secret information to the British.

Secret Letters

Arnold began sending secret letters to Major John André, a British Army officer. Arnold told André where American troops were located and where they stored their supplies. This is called **treason**. Arnold also demanded that the British pay him for this information.

But Arnold managed to keep his spying a secret. He was even given command of a military base called West Point. But instead of making West Point strong, he made it weaker.

Then he met with André and gave him plans that would allow the British to take West Point. Arnold was going to give the base to the enemy!

Busted!

Everything changed the very next day, when André was captured by American soldiers. He was carrying the plans from Arnold. It was proof that Arnold was a spy!

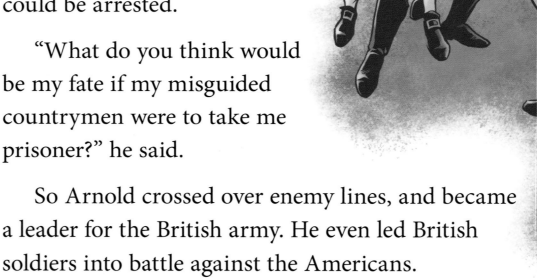

Arnold escaped before he could be arrested.

"What do you think would be my fate if my misguided countrymen were to take me prisoner?" he said.

So Arnold crossed over enemy lines, and became a leader for the British army. He even led British soldiers into battle against the Americans.

Arnold's bad deeds did not help the British win the war. The Americans eventually won and earned their independence.

But to this day, to call someone a "Benedict Arnold" is the same as calling them a traitor.

Tributes to Benedict Arnold

Even though many people think of Arnold as a bad guy, there are some tributes to his successes in battle. At the site of the Saratoga battle, there is a monument of Arnold's boot that reads "In memory of the most brilliant soldier of the Continental army, who was desperately wounded on this spot, winning for his countrymen the decisive battle of the American Revolution." There are also plaques for Arnold at the United States Military Academy at West Point. None of the tributes, however, include Arnold's name!

Final Regrets?

Arnold lived the rest of his life in England. No one knows for sure if he ever felt guilty about **betraying** the Americans. Legend has it that right before he died, he requested to wear his old American military uniform.

"Let me die in this old uniform in which I fought my battles," he said, according to the legend. "May God forgive me for ever having put on another."

Glossary

betraying exposing one's country to danger by giving information to the enemy

businessman someone with a specific set of skills for a certain job

captain the person in command

Continental Congress the group of people who made the laws for the thirteen colonies during the American Revolution

evacuate to be removed from danger to a safe place

expedition a long journey with a particular purpose

filed turning in official documents to the government or military leaders

general a commander of an army

historian an expert in history

independence being free from control of another country

molasses dark brown syrup used in baking

organization a group of people who come together for a particular purpose

outgunned when the other side has more weapons, or better weapons

powder house place where gunpowder and other supplies are stored

promotion raising someone to a higher rank

stash something that is stored secretly and safely away

taxes money you have to pay to the government

treason the crime of betraying one's country

withdraw to leave a particular place

For More Information

Books

Gunderson, Jessica. *Benedict Arnold: Battlefield Hero or Selfish Traitor?* (Perspectives on History) Capstone Press, 2013.

Burgan, Michael. *Benedict Arnold: American Hero and Traitor.* (Graphic Biographies) Capstone Press,. 2007.

Sheinkin, Steve. *The Notorious Benedict Arnold: A True Story of Adventure, Heroism & Treachery.* Square Fish, 2013.

Places

Boot Monument to Benedict Arnold's leg, Saratoga National Historic Park, Stillwater, New York.

Treason site of Benedict Arnold (where Arnold met with British Major John André), Haverstraw, New York.

Patriot's Park (where André was captured and Arnold's treason was discovered), Sleepy Hollow/Tarrytown, New York.

Index

About the Author and Illustrator

Aaron Derr is a writer based just outside of Dallas, Texas. He has more than 15 years of experience writing and editing magazines and books for kids of all ages. When he's not reading or writing, Aaron enjoys watching and playing sports, and doing pretty much anything with his wife and two kids.

Scott R. Brooks started a career in full-time illustration several years ago. Scott shares his Atlanta, GA studio with his illustrator wife, Karen. They share their home with their 2 clever children, and their somewhat less clever dog and cat.